I Have a Dollar

By Jeri Cipriano

Scott Foresman
is an imprint of

Glenview, Illinois • Boston, Massachusetts • Chandler, Arizona •
Upper Saddle River, New Jersey

Photographs

Every effort has been made to secure permission and provide appropriate credit for photographic material. The publisher deeply regrets any omission and pledges to correct errors called to its attention in subsequent editions.

Unless otherwise acknowledged, all photographs are the property of Pearson Education, Inc.

Photo locators denoted as follows: Top (T), Center (C), Bottom (B), Left (L), Right (R), Background (Bkgd)

ISBN 13: 978-0-328-46378-7
ISBN 10:   0-328-46378-7

3 4 5 6 7 8 9 10 V010 14 13 12 11 10

I have a dollar.

I will buy a book.

I have a dollar.

I will buy a plant.

I have a dollar.

I will buy a flower.

I have a dollar.

I will buy some balloons.

I have a dollar.

I will buy some apples.

I have a dollar.
I will save it!